W9-BQA-837

THIS BOOK BELONGS TO:

....

....

My 52 Lists project

Journaling Inspiration for KIDS!

BY MOOREA SEAL

SASQUATCH BOOKS
SEATTLE

FOR MATHEW, AVI, AND NEOMA.
Being your Auntie Moomoo has made
me happier than just about anything in
the universe. I will love you and accept
all that you are, no matter what.

Hey you! In this journal, you will find 52 lists to fill out, have fun with, and discover more about yourself. This is your fun, free space to write, scribble, dream, and make your very own.

Do you like collecting things? In this journal, you get to do exactly that. Collect and record all of the special stuff that makes you who you are right now—like a time capsule of you! There are no right or wrong answers!

Since there are 52 lists in this journal and 52 weeks in a year, you could fill in one list a week, choosing a special day each week to journal. Or you can do as many as you want, whenever you want, in whatever order you want! This is your journal—how you use it is completely up to you.

Grown-ups! Visit **52ListsProject.com/Grownups-guide** for a guide to using this journal with the kids in your life.

Contents

LIST 1: List the things you want to do this year. 12

LIST 2: List your favorite characters from books, movies, TV shows, and other media. 14

LIST 3: List the things that make you happy! 16

LIST 4: List your favorite songs. 18

LIST 5: Circle the ideas that are most important to you. 21

LIST 6: List the ways you love to have fun! 22

LIST 7: List all the people who brighten your day. 24

LIST 8: Create your bucket list! What do you want to try, see, and experience in your lifetime? 26

LIST 9: List everything that is special to you. 29

LIST 10: If you were a superhero, what superpowers would you have? List what you would do with your powers. 32

LIST 11: List the animals that remind you of each of these feelings. 34

LIST 12: List the things that make you laugh.   **36**

LIST 13: List the talents you would like to have and
how you can practice them.   **40**

LIST 14: List the people you want to be like.   **42**

LIST 15: List the adventures you want to have.   **45**

LIST 16: List what your dream house would be like.   **48**

LIST 17: List your funniest memories.   **51**

LIST 18: Close your eyes. List all of the sounds that
you hear while they are closed.   **54**

LIST 19: Circle all of the ways you like to play./List
your favorite play activities.   **56**

LIST 20: List what makes you feel free.   **58**

LIST 21: List the things you want to make.   **62**

LIST 22: List your favorite places.   **64**

LIST 23: Don't even worry about words this week.
Draw, scribble, or color how you are feeling right now.   **67**

LIST 24: List movies, games, people, places, anything you think is really cool. 70

LIST 25: List the things you like about people you know. 72

LIST 26: List the things you would change in your life if you could. 74

LIST 27: List the things that make you feel healthy and strong. 76

LIST 28: List all the things you see around you right now. 80

LIST 29: List the jobs you want to try when you are older. 82

LIST 30: List everything you can think of that is your favorite color./Draw some things in your favorite color. 85

LIST 31: List the words that describe who you are. 88

LIST 32: List the things you would tell yourself when you were just five years old. 90

LIST 33: List what you want your life to be like when you are twenty-five years old. 92

LIST 34: List where you would go and what you would do if you could drive a car. 96

LIST 35: List the things that feel challenging to you. 98

LIST 36: List everything you love to do outdoors. 100

LIST 37: List what you would spend one hundred dollars on, just for you. 104

LIST 38: List the ways you take care of yourself.   **106**

LIST 39: List the most beautiful things you have ever seen.   **109**

LIST 40: List the places you would like to visit and explore!   **112**

LIST 41: List your favorite things about each season.   **114**

LIST 42: List the things that make you feel calm.   **118**

LIST 43: List your favorite things to eat and drink.   **120**

LIST 44: Circle which of the options feel most like you.   **123**

LIST 45: List your favorite holidays.   **124**

LIST 46: List the things that make you feel safe and strong.   **126**

LIST 47: List the things you are thankful for.   **130**

LIST 48: List what the following emotions feel like in your body.   **132**

LIST 49: List your favorite stories found in books, movies, TV, video games, and more.   **134**

LIST 50: List the things you couldn't do when you were little but you can do now.   **138**

LIST 51: List the things you want to be known for.   **140**

LIST 52: List your favorite memories from this year.   **142**

List 1

LIST THE THINGS YOU WANT TO DO THIS YEAR.

_____

_____

_____

_____

_____

_____

_____

_____

List 2

LIST YOUR FAVORITE CHARACTERS FROM BOOKS,
MOVIES, TV SHOWS, AND OTHER MEDIA.

List 3

LIST THE THINGS THAT MAKE YOU HAPPY!

_____

_____

_____

_____

_____

_____

_____

_____

_____

_____

_____

_____

List 4

LIST YOUR FAVORITE SONGS.

_____

_____

_____

_____

_____

_____

_____

_____

_____

_____

List 5

CIRCLE THE IDEAS THAT ARE MOST
IMPORTANT TO YOU.

PEACE   ADVENTURE

INDEPENDENCE   CURIOSITY

FRIENDSHIP   SHARING

LAUGHTER   COMFORT

LOVE   SUCCESS

ART   HAPPINESS

AFFECTION   FREEDOM

CONFIDENCE   FAMILY

KINDNESS   NATURE

BELIEF   HOME

PRIVACY   BRAVERY

MONEY   DREAMS

SELF-EXPRESSION

List 6

LIST THE WAYS YOU LOVE TO HAVE FUN!

List 7

LIST ALL THE PEOPLE WHO BRIGHTEN YOUR DAY.

List 8

CREATE YOUR BUCKET LIST! WHAT DO YOU WANT
TO TRY, SEE, AND EXPERIENCE IN YOUR LIFETIME?

List 9

LIST EVERYTHING THAT IS SPECIAL TO YOU.

_____

_____

_____

_____

_____

_____

_____

_____

_____

_____

_____

List 10

IF YOU WERE A SUPERHERO, WHAT SUPERPOWERS
WOULD YOU HAVE? LIST WHAT YOU WOULD DO
WITH YOUR POWERS.

List 11

LIST THE ANIMALS THAT REMIND YOU OF
EACH OF THESE FEELINGS.

STRONG: _____

CONFUSED: _____

ANNOYING: _____

LOVING: _____

SMART: _____

ANGRY: _____

FUNNY: _____

SAD: _____

WISE: _____

EMBARRASSED: _____

SNEAKY: _____

HAPPY: _____

CREATIVE: _____

ANXIOUS: _____

POWERFUL: _____

SCARED: _____

UNIQUE: _____

GENTLE: _____

FRUSTRATED: _____

WILD: _____

List 12

LIST THE THINGS THAT MAKE YOU LAUGH.

List 13

LIST THE TALENTS YOU WOULD LIKE TO HAVE AND
HOW YOU CAN PRACTICE THEM.

List 14

LIST THE PEOPLE YOU WANT TO BE LIKE.

List 15

LIST THE ADVENTURES YOU WANT TO HAVE.

_____

_____

_____

_____

_____

_____

_____

_____

_____

_____

_____

_____

List 16

LIST WHAT YOUR DREAM HOUSE WOULD BE LIKE.

(MAYBE IT'S A TREEHOUSE, A SPACESHIP, OR SOMETHING ELSE UNIQUE! USE YOUR IMAGINATION.)

List 17

LIST YOUR FUNNIEST MEMORIES.

_____

_____

_____

_____

_____

_____

_____

_____

_____

_____

_____

List 18

CLOSE YOUR EYES. LIST ALL OF THE SOUNDS THAT
YOU HEAR WHILE THEY ARE CLOSED.

*(YOU'LL PROBABLY NEED TO OPEN YOUR EYES TO WRITE
DOWN WHAT YOU HEAR.)*

List 19

CIRCLE ALL OF THE WAYS YOU LIKE TO PLAY.

BY MYSELF

FOLLOWING THE LEAD OF SOMEONE ELSE

LEADING AN ACTIVITY

DOING MY OWN THING BUT BEING NEAR
MY FRIENDS AND FAMILY

BUILDING AND CREATING A GAME WITH A CLOSE
FRIEND OR SOMEONE NEW

PRETENDING TO BE A CHARACTER FROM A STORY

LEARNING A NEW SKILL OR TRYING A
NEW ACTIVITY

TAKING SOMETHING APART TO UNDERSTAND
HOW IT WORKS

TELLING STORIES AND LISTENING TO THEM

MAKING MUSIC, DANCING, OR CREATING ART

EXPLORING THE OUTDOORS

HAVING FUN IN AND WITH MY IMAGINATION

LIST YOUR FAVORITE PLAY ACTIVITIES.

List 20

LIST WHAT MAKES YOU FEEL FREE.

List 21

LIST THE THINGS YOU WANT TO MAKE.

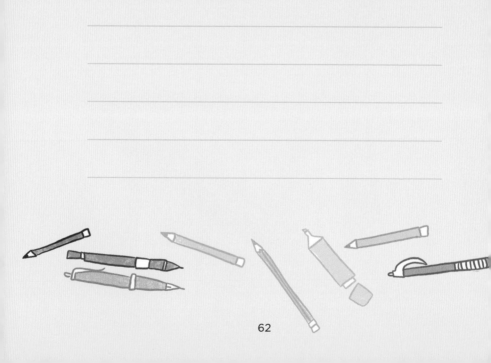

List 22

LIST YOUR FAVORITE PLACES.

List 23

DON'T EVEN WORRY ABOUT WORDS THIS WEEK.
DRAW, SCRIBBLE, OR COLOR HOW YOU ARE
FEELING RIGHT NOW.

*(GET AS MESSY AS YOU WANT—EVEN TEAR OUT AND
CRUMPLE THE PAGE IF YOU LIKE!)*

List 24

LIST MOVIES, GAMES, PEOPLE, PLACES, ANYTHING
YOU THINK IS REALLY COOL.

_____

_____

_____

_____

_____

_____

_____

_____

_____

_____

_____

_____

List 25

LIST THE THINGS YOU LIKE ABOUT
PEOPLE YOU KNOW.

List 26

LIST THE THINGS YOU WOULD CHANGE IN YOUR
LIFE IF YOU COULD.

List 27

LIST THE THINGS THAT MAKE YOU FEEL
HEALTHY AND STRONG.

List 28

LIST ALL THE THINGS YOU SEE AROUND YOU
RIGHT NOW.

List 29

LIST THE JOBS YOU WANT TO TRY
WHEN YOU ARE OLDER.

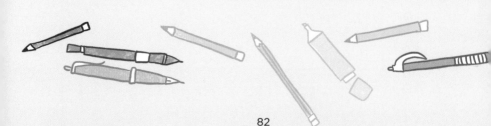

List 30

LIST EVERYTHING YOU CAN THINK OF THAT IS
YOUR FAVORITE COLOR.

_____

_____

_____

_____

_____

_____

_____

_____

_____

_____

DRAW SOME THINGS IN YOUR FAVORITE COLOR.

List 31

LIST THE WORDS THAT DESCRIBE WHO YOU ARE.

List 32

LIST THE THINGS YOU WOULD TELL YOURSELF
WHEN YOU WERE JUST FIVE YEARS OLD.

List 33

LIST WHAT YOU WANT YOUR LIFE TO BE LIKE
WHEN YOU ARE TWENTY-FIVE YEARS OLD.

_____

_____

_____

_____

_____

_____

_____

_____

List 34

LIST WHERE YOU WOULD GO AND WHAT YOU
WOULD DO IF YOU COULD DRIVE A CAR.

_____

_____

_____

_____

_____

_____

_____

_____

List 35

LIST THE THINGS THAT FEEL
CHALLENGING TO YOU.

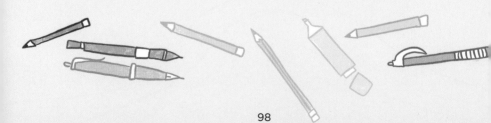

List 36

LIST EVERYTHING YOU LOVE TO
DO OUTDOORS.

List 37

LIST WHAT YOU WOULD SPEND ONE HUNDRED
DOLLARS ON, JUST FOR YOU.

_____

_____

_____

_____

_____

_____

_____

_____

_____

_____

List 38

LIST THE WAYS YOU TAKE CARE OF YOURSELF.

List 39

LIST THE MOST BEAUTIFUL THINGS
YOU HAVE EVER SEEN.

List 40

LIST THE PLACES YOU WOULD LIKE TO
VISIT AND EXPLORE!

List 41

LIST YOUR FAVORITE THINGS
ABOUT EACH SEASON.

SPRING:

SUMMER:

FALL: _____

_____

_____

_____

_____

_____

WINTER: _____

_____

_____

_____

_____

_____

List 42

LIST THE THINGS THAT MAKE YOU FEEL CALM.

List 43

LIST YOUR FAVORITE THINGS TO EAT AND DRINK.

List 44

CIRCLE WHICH OF THE OPTIONS FEEL
MOST LIKE YOU.

SWEET or SALTY?

PLAYING INSIDE or OUTSIDE?

BEACH, VALLEY, or MOUNTAIN?

DOGS or CATS?

ORGANIZED or MESSY AND WILD?

OUTGOING or SHY?

SPRING, SUMMER, FALL, or WINTER?

CALM or ENERGETIC?

NIGHTTIME or MORNING?

STAY THE SAME or OFTEN CHANGE?

EXPERIMENT or FOLLOW THE RULES?

PLAYFUL or SERIOUS?

SLOW or FAST?

PAST, PRESENT, or FUTURE?

TOGETHER or ALONE?

EASY or CHALLENGING?

FANTASY or REALITY?

EARTH, FIRE, WATER, or AIR?

START or FINISH?

LEADER or SIDEKICK?

SUNSHINE, CLOUDS, RAIN, or SNOW?

List 45

LIST YOUR FAVORITE HOLIDAYS.

List 46

LIST THE THINGS THAT MAKE YOU FEEL
SAFE AND STRONG.

List 47

LIST THE THINGS YOU ARE THANKFUL FOR.

List 48

LIST WHAT THE FOLLOWING EMOTIONS
FEEL LIKE IN YOUR BODY.

WHEN I AM HAPPY, MY BODY FEELS . . . ———————————

———————————————————————————————————

———————————————————————————————————

———————————————————————————————————

WHEN I AM SAD, MY BODY FEELS . . . ———————————

———————————————————————————————————

———————————————————————————————————

———————————————————————————————————

WHEN I AM MAD, MY BODY FEELS . . . ———————————

———————————————————————————————————

———————————————————————————————————

———————————————————————————————————

WHEN I AM EXCITED, MY BODY FEELS . . . _____

_____

_____

_____

WHEN I AM NERVOUS, MY BODY FEELS . . . _____

_____

_____

_____

WHEN I AM CALM, MY BODY FEELS . . . _____

_____

_____

_____

List 49

LIST YOUR FAVORITE STORIES FOUND IN BOOKS,
MOVIES, TV, VIDEO GAMES, AND MORE.

List 50

LIST THE THINGS YOU COULDN'T DO WHEN YOU
WERE LITTLE BUT YOU CAN DO NOW.

List 51

LIST THE THINGS YOU WANT TO BE KNOWN FOR.

List 52

LIST YOUR FAVORITE MEMORIES FROM THIS YEAR.

(THE FINAL LIST!)

MOOREA SEAL is a Seattle-based author, speaker, and designer, as well as an avid list maker with over one million books, journals, and stationery products in print. Her passion lies in giving voice to the wise mind and inner child that live within us all and providing resources for happiness, resilience, and self-expression. She finds hope in transparency and believes that to truly love and empower others, we must seek to accept and express our own true selves. Join her community at **MooreaSeal.com**.

Manufactured in China by C&C Offset Printing Co. Ltd.
Shenzhen, Guangdong Province, in May 2021

Editor: Hannah Elnan | Production editor: Bridget Sweet
Design: Anna Goldstein | Illustrations: Moorea Seal

Illustrated type: Julia Manchik (cover and list heads), © Shutterstock /Sveta Evglevskaia (pages 10–11), © Shutterstock/Hasenkamp26.de (pages 78–79), © Shutterstock/kamilla_writes_letters (pages 102–103), © Shutterstock/Alice Vacca (pages 136–137)

Photographs: Arielle Vey (front cover and pages 2–4, 28, 50, 53, 102–103, 108, 111, 116–117, 128–129, 136–137), © iStock.com/kyoshino (cover notebook), Sergey Pesterev (pages 10–11), © iStock/Bogdan Kurylo (page 20), © iStock /caracterdesign (page 31), Drew Beamer (pages 38–39), Josh Hild (page 44), Hello I'm Nik (page 47), Jan Antonin Kolar (pages 60–61), © Shutterstock /Africa Studio (page 66), Dewang Gupta (page 69), Wesley Tingey (pages 78–79), Mockaroon (page 84), Mihai Surdu (page 87), © Dejan Ristovski / Stocksy United (pages 94–95), Tim Mossholder (page 122), © Shutterstock/Stanislav Savin (back cover)

SASQUATCH BOOKS with colophon is a registered trademark of Penguin Random House LLC

25 24 23 22 21   9 8 7 6 5 4 3 2 1

ISBN: 978-1-63217-394-2

Sasquatch Books | 1904 Third Avenue, Suite 710
Seattle, WA 98101

SasquatchBooks.com